HOW TO DRAW

Faces

by Kathryn Clay

illustrated by Anne Timmons

Capstone press

Mankato, Minnesota

Snap Books are published by Capstone Press,
151 Good Counsel Drive, P.O. Box 669, Mankato, Minnesota 56002.
www.capstonepress.com

Books published by Capstone Press are manufactured with paper
containing at least 10 percent post-consumer waste.

Library of Congress Cataloging-in-Publication Data
Clay, Kathryn.
    How to draw faces / by Kathryn Clay; illustrated by Anne Timmons.
    p. cm. — (Snap books. Drawing fun)
    Includes bibliographical references and index.
    Summary: "Lively text and fun illustrations describe how to draw faces" — Provided by publisher.
    ISBN 978-1-4296-3404-5 (library binding)
    1. Face in art. 2. Drawing — Technique. I. Timmons, Anne. II. Title. III. Series.
NC770.C6 2010   2009001579
743.4'9 — dc22

Credits
Juliette Peters, designer
Abbey Fitzgerald, colorist

Photo Credits
Capstone Press/TJ Thoraldson Digital Photography, 4 (pencil), 5 (all), 32 (pencil)

The author dedicates this book to Andy, Betsy, Joel, and Kari.

Table of Contents

Getting Started

Take a close look at your face. Have you ever noticed all the different shapes? These shapes help to make each face unique. They're also the keys to drawing different types of faces. It doesn't matter if the face is old, young, silly, or scary. While drawing facial features can be tricky, it's not impossible.

Start by drawing a big egg shape on your paper. Add round eyes, oval ears, a triangle nose, and a heart-shaped mouth. That's all you need for a basic face. But if you picked up this book, you want to draw more than a basic face. Maybe you'd like to draw your friend as a funny cartoon? Then you'll want to check out how to draw a caricature. If you'd like to sketch your favorite celebrity, take a look at the pop star profile. With your skills and the instructions in this book, every face can become an exciting work of art.

Of course, this book can't show you how to draw every kind of face. There are just too many! But once you've mastered some of the faces in this book, you'll be able to draw all kinds of faces. Let your imagination run wild, and see what kinds of cool faces you can create.

Must-Have Materials

1. First you'll need something to draw on. Any blank, white paper will work well.

2. Pencils are a must for these drawing projects. Be sure to keep a bunch nearby.

3. Because sharp pencils make clean lines, you'll be sharpening those pencils a lot. Have a pencil sharpener handy.

4. Even the best artist needs to erase a line now and then. Pencil erasers wear out fast. A rubber or kneaded eraser will last much longer.

5. To make your drawings pop off the page, use colored pencils or markers.

Face First

Here are the face basics that will help you with the projects in this book. Notice how this girl's eyes are halfway between the top of the head and the chin. So are her ears. Her nose fills the space between the eyes. After drawing the basics, add all the extras that make each face unique. For this girl, that means drawing lots of curly hair.

Faces can be all different shapes. Try drawing this face as a rectangle, heart, circle, or triangle.

STEP 1

STEP 2

STEP 3

STEP 4

Pop Star Profile

Get ready to capture this pop star's best side. A profile shows just one side of the face, so it's a great choice for budding artists. You only need to draw one eye, and the nose and mouth are simple outlines. When you've finished the face, add a microphone to the drawing. Now your pop star is ready to rock out.

After mastering this singer, try drawing his backup band.

STEP 1

STEP 2

STEP 3

STEP 4

Happy Baby

Babies naturally attract a lot of attention. That's why artists of all ages love to draw them. If you're drawing a happy baby, focus on the eyes and the mouth. The eyes should be wide and curious. The mouth should reveal a big smile.

Try drawing the rest of the baby. Don't forget tiny fingers and toes.

STEP 1

STEP 2

STEP 3

STEP 4

11

Old Man

As people age, their faces change. Skin gets wrinkly and hair might thin. Eyeglasses become an important accessory. To draw this old man, start with a basic face. Then draw short, narrow lines around the eyes and forehead for wrinkles. Complete the face with two big, bushy eyebrows.

Try drawing this old man chatting with an old woman.

STEP 1

STEP 2

STEP 3

STEP 4

13

Villain

Villains are always up to no good, and you can tell that by their faces. To make this bad guy look especially sneaky, his face should be full of sharp lines. That means a pointy chin and super-arched eyebrows. Add a mustache that he can twirl while thinking about his next top secret stunt.

Once you've completed the villain, try sketching his sneaky sidekick.

STEP 1

STEP 2

STEP 3

STEP 4

Superhero

Evildoers beware! This superhero's smile can hypnotize even the toughest bad guy. But don't let her sweet expression fool you. She uses her superhuman strength to keep criminals off the streets. To keep this modest superhero's true identity secret, draw a dark mask around her eyes.

Try drawing this superhero fighting the evil villain on page 14.

STEP 1

STEP 2

STEP 3

STEP 4

Pirate

Arrr! This pirate doesn't need a beard or an eye patch to sail the South Sea. Instead, draw her wearing a rounded bicorne hat complete with skull and crossbones. Then draw a pet parrot to accompany her on long sea voyages.

Try drawing a crew of pirates digging up buried treasure.

STEP 1

STEP 2

STEP 3

STEP 4

Manga Girl

Manga is a type of comic drawing that started in Japan. Manga characters have distinct facial features. Large eyes and pointed chins are common features. So are small noses, simple mouths, and spiky hair. This manga girl has all these features and a fierce attitude to match.

Give this manga girl a new hairstyle. Draw long hair pulled into a ponytail or short pigtails on the top of her head.

STEP 1

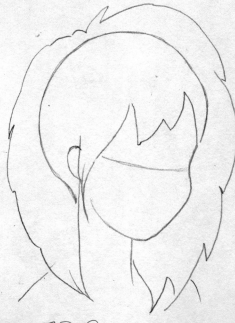

STEP 2

STEP 3

STEP 4

Picasso Abstract

Famous artist Pablo Picasso (1881–1973) drew faces with crazy colors and shapes. He used an abstract style to create paintings now worth millions of dollars. Try creating your own abstract portrait. Draw a face with mismatched facial features and bright colors. Your drawing doesn't have to look realistic, but it should resemble a face.

Abstract style can be used to draw almost anything. Try drawing an abstract tree or car.

STEP 1

STEP 2

STEP 3

STEP 4

Caricature

If your subject has a sense of humor, try drawing him or her as a caricature. Caricatures are cartoon-like portraits that highlight someone's distinct facial features. This guy's caricature includes round, fat cheeks, tiny ears, and a toothy grin.

Try drawing a caricature of someone you know by finding his or her distinct features. Draw your dad's big nose or your mom's curly hair.

STEP 1

STEP 2

STEP 3

STEP 4

Family Portrait

Now that you've practiced several faces, get ready to draw one big, happy family. It's not difficult if you take it step-by-step. Start by drawing the dad. Then add the mom and son. Next draw the daughter. And don't forget about the family pooch.

Do you have a baby brother or a new kitten? Try drawing a portrait of your unique family.

STEP 1

STEP 2

STEP 3

To finish this drawing, turn to the next page. ➡

STEP 4

STEP 5

abstract (AB-strakt) — based on ideas rather than things; abstract paintings show impressions rather than what people or objects actually look like.

bicorne (BY-korn) — a hat with the brim turned up on two sides

caricature (KAR-ih-kuh-chur) — an exaggerated, funny drawing of someone

distinct (diss-TINGKT) — unique and clearly different

hypnotize (HIP-nuh-tize) — to put another person in a sleeplike state

manga (MAHN-gah) — a style of art used in comic books or graphic novel from Japan

profile (PROH-file) — a side view or drawing of someone's head

unique (yoo-NEEK) — one of a kind

Read More

Clay, Kathryn. *How to Draw Cool Kids.* Drawing Fun. Mankato, Minn.: Capstone Press, 2009.

Court, Rob. *How to Draw Faces.* How-to-Draw Books. Chanhassen, Minn.: Child's World, 2005.

Yaun, Debra Kauffman. *Faces and Features: Learn to Draw Step by Step.* Laguna Hills, Calif.: Walter Foster, 2006.

Internet Sites

FactHound offers a safe, fun way to find Internet sites related to this book. All of the sites on FactHound have been researched by our staff.

Here's all you do:

Visit *www.facthound.com*

FactHound will fetch the best sites for you!

Index